THE BEST
CATS
EVER

AMERICAN SHORTHAIRS ARE THE BEST!

Elaine Landau

LERNER PUBLICATIONS COMPANY · MINNEAPOLIS

Lerner Publications Company
A division of Lerner Publishing Group, Inc.
241 First Avenue North
Minneapolis, MN 55401 U.S.A.

Website address: www.lernerbooks.com

Library of Congress Cataloging-in-Publication Data

Landau, Elaine.
     American shorthairs are the best! / by Elaine Landau.
        p.   cm. — (The best cats ever)
     Includes index.
     ISBN 978-0-7613-6430-6 (lib. bdg. : alk. paper)
     1. American shorthair cat—Juvenile literature. I. Title.
   SF449.A45L36 2011
   636.8'22—dc22   2010024223

Manufactured in the United States of America
1 — CG — 12/31/10

TABLE OF CONTENTS

CHAPTER ONE

THE IDEAL CAT

Meet an all-American cat. This cat is fun and friendly.
It likes people and even gets along with dogs.
It's easy to fall for this pretty kitty.
It's an **American shorthair.**

This American shorthair loves to have its picture taken!

Solid and Sturdy

American shorthairs are medium- to large-sized cats. Males can weigh as much as 15 pounds (7 kilograms). Females may weigh up to 12 pounds (5 kg).

These cats have stocky, muscular bodies. They are strong and athletic. And American shorthairs are cute as can be. They have round heads and full cheeks. This gives them a supersweet look.

Cats of Many Colors

An American shorthair is, indeed, short-haired. Bet you guessed that from its name. Its coat tends to be thick and glossy.

NAME THAT CAT!

Are you about to get the best cat ever? Then you're going to need the best NAME ever for that kitty. See if you like any of these.

Pandora Theo SIMON

Ariella

FELIX Isis

Lucy

LiLy Gizmo Winston

But American shorthairs don't all look alike. Picking an American shorthair is like picking a flavor in an ice-cream store. These cats come in more than eighty different colors and patterns. You're sure to find one you like.

American shorthairs come in a variety of colors and patterns. Which one do you like the best?

But two types are most common. One has black stripes on a silver background. The other has black stripes on a brown background. Some people say their stripes make them look like tiny tigers!

The color patterns on American shorthairs sometimes make them look like baby tigers!

A Fun Playmate

American shorthairs are a
joy to own. They are active
and curious. It's fun to
watch them explore things.

These cats also like being around humans. But please be warned. If you get an American shorthair, it will want to spend some time on your lap.

Chasing balls and catching toys are fun games for American shorthairs.

These cute kitties also love to play. They enjoy toys and have lots of energy. They'll want you to play with them whenever you can. Who'll have more fun—you or your cat?

American shorthair owners think they have the best cats ever. It's hard to disagree. American shorthairs seem to be nearly purrfect pussycats.

A realistic mouse toy will drive your American Shorthair wild!

11

HOW THE BREED GOT STARTED

The American shorthair is no stranger to our shores. These kitties have been here for almost four hundred years. They came to North America with the early colonists.

Early colonists brought American shorthairs to North America. This engraving was created in 1713.

Working Cats

Ships sailing from Europe to North America often had cats on board. Those cats weren't pets. Instead, they had an important job to do. They reduced the number of rats and mice on the ships. Those rodents meant trouble. They could get into the ships' food supply.

When the colonists arrived in North America, they kept the cats. These frisky, short-haired felines were good mousers. They went after rats and mice in barns and fields. They also chased away squirrels that fed on the colonists' corn.

Cats had important jobs on ships—keeping rats and mice out of the food.

PLAGUE FIGHTERS

In the early 1900s, the plague broke out in San Francisco, California. Rats were spreading the deadly disease. People brought lots of cats to the city to get rid of the rats. Can you guess what kind of cat got the job done? It was the American shorthair.

Pretty Fine Pets

At first, these cats had to work for their keep. But as the years passed, things changed. People began to want them as pets. They liked the American shorthair's good looks and pleasant manner. These pretty kitties also began to win ribbons in pet shows. In time, American shorthairs became one of the country's favorite breeds.

CATS OF THE PAST

The ancient Egyptians valued cats highly. They made it a crime to harm or kill a cat. The Egyptian goddess Bast (right) had the head of a cat and the body of a woman.

The American shorthair has been a hit in other places too. These cats are very well liked in Japan and other parts of Asia. They have been ranked as the eighth most popular cat in the world.

THE RIGHT CAT FOR YOU?

Who wouldn't want an all-American kitty? Every home should have an American shorthair, right? Of course not! They make wonderful pets. But they aren't right for everyone. Read on to see if this breed is the right pet for you.

Home Alone

Are you very busy? Do you have lots of after-school activities? Are you out with friends most weekends? Do the adults in your family work outside the home? If so, an American shorthair might not be the best choice for you.

American shorthairs like to be with their owners.

These cats don't like being left home alone for long periods. And sometimes they let you know.

American shorthairs need to be with people. They like being part of the household's activities. These cats should not be home alone for long periods. If you're not home much, a bird or a fish might be a better choice for you.

Unlike fish, American Shorthairs need lots of "people" time.

Costly Kitties

An American shorthair is a purebred pussycat. These kittens are quite costly. Breeders want hundreds of dollars for them. Can you afford a high-priced pet? Be sure to discuss this with your family before you fall for one of these pretty kitties.

RESCUE AN AMERICAN SHORTHAIR!

Can't afford a costly kitten? Then how about getting an older cat? You can find an older American shorthair at rescue centers for this breed. American shorthairs have long lives, so you'll still have years of fun ahead. Often these older cats are given to good homes for a small fee. But remember that you and your family will still have to pay for food, health care, and pet supplies.

On the Plus Side

American shorthairs do well with most families. They get along with both kids and older folks. They are usually fine with other household pets too. These cats really enjoy being part of a family.

NICE TO HAVE AROUND

The American shorthair is not one of those fussy, picky pussycats. It enjoys all sorts of family activities. Its pleasant manner makes it a good choice for many people.

Have you decided if an American shorthair is the right pet for you? If it is, you've made a super choice. You've picked a wonderful pussycat. Get set for tons of fun! A great kitty is coming your way.

Most American shorthairs like to be petted.

CHAPTER FOUR

HOME AT LAST

The day you've waited for has come at last. Your American shorthair is finally coming home.

These tiny kitties are curious. They want to explore their new home.

Make this a super day for your cat too. You'll want your new pet to feel comfortable. Be sure to have the supplies you'll need. This basic list is a good place to start:

- food and water bowls

- cat food

- litter box

- kitty litter

- brush and wide-tooth steel comb

- scratching post

- cat carrier

See a Vet Soon!

A veterinarian, or vet, is a doctor who takes care of animals. Take your new cat to a vet right away. During the visit, the vet will check your cat's health. Your American shorthair will also get the shots it needs to stay well.

Take your kitty back to the vet for checkups. Also, take your cat to the vet if it gets sick.

A vet can help keep your American Shorthair healthy.

Feeding Kitty

Ask your vet what to feed your American shorthair, and stick to that diet. Don't give your cat snacks. Not even a slice of your birthday cake or a scoop of ice cream on a warm day. American shorthairs tend to overeat, and this can lead to an unhealthy weight gain.

WHAT'S AS IMPORTANT AS FOOD?

You hear a lot about different cat foods, but water is just as important for your pet. Make sure your cat always has fresh water in a clean bowl. It's a must for your cat's good health.

Good Grooming

Lucky you! An American shorthair does not need a lot of grooming. You can skip the trips to kitty beauty salons. Just brush and comb your cat's coat once a week. This removes any loose or dead hair.

A brush like this one will keep your cat's coat nice and shiny.

Question: Who has better hearing—humans or cats?

Answer: Cats hear better than people. Cats also have better eyesight than you and a better sense of smell.

You and Your American Shorthair

You can count on your cat to be your best friend. It will always be there for you. Make sure you are there for it as well. That means feeding and petting it even when you'd rather be doing other things.

These cats love to be in the middle of the action—even when it's homework!

GLOSSARY

breed: a particular type of cat. Cats of the same breed have the same body shape and general features. *Breed* can also refer to producing kittens.

breeder: someone who mates cats to produce a particular kind of cat

coat: a cat's fur

diet: the food your cat eats

feline: a cat, or having to do with cats

groom: to brush, clean, and trim a cat's coat

purebred: a cat whose parents are the same breed

rescue center: a shelter where stray and abandoned cats are kept until they are adopted

veterinarian: a doctor who treats animals. Veterinarians are called vets for short.

FOR MORE INFORMATION

Books

Brecke, Nicole, and Patricia M. Stockland. *Cats You Can Draw*. Minneapolis: Millbrook Press, 2010. Perfect for cat lovers, this colorful book teaches readers how to draw many popular cat breeds.

Brown, Ruth. *Gracie the Lighthouse Cat*. London: Andersen Press, 2011. Gracie the lighthouse cat and Grace Darling, the lighthouse keeper's daughter, both have an adventure one very windy night.

Furstinger, Nancy. *American Shorthair Cats*. Edina, MN: ABDO, 2005. This easy-to-read book provides information on buying and living with an American shorthair cat.

Harris, Trudy. *Tally Cat Keeps Track*. Minneapolis: Millbrook Press, 2011. Tally McNally is a cat who loves to tally—but one day, he gets into a jam. Will his friends find a way to help him?

Landau, Elaine. *Ragdoll Cats Are the Best!* Minneapolis: Lerner Publications Company, 2011. Learn about another cute, cuddly cat breed.

Landau, Elaine. *Your Pet Cat*. Rev. ed. New York: Children's Press, 2007. This title is a good guide for young people on choosing and caring for a cat.

Websites

ASPCA Kids
http://www.aspca.org/aspcakids
Check out this website for helpful hints on caring for a cat and other pets.

For Kids: About Cats
http://kids.cfa.org
Be sure to visit this website for kids on cats and cat shows. Don't miss the link to some fun games as well.

LERNER *e* SOURCE™
Expand learning beyond the printed book. Download free, complementary educational resources for this book from our website, www.lerneresource.com

Index

Photo Acknowledgments

The images in this book are used with the permission of: © Photo by Helmi Flick, p. 4; © Photos by Chanan, pp. 5, 6, 6–7, 8 (top), 24–25, 28 (top); © iStockphoto.com/Chanyut Sribua-rawd, p. 8 (bottom); © Brian Kimball/www.kimballstock.com, p. 9; © Fiona Green, pp. 10, 11 (top), 14 (left), 15, 17, 18 (top), 20, 21, 25, 27, 28 (bottom), 29; © Eyewave/Dreamstime.com, p. 11 (bottom); © Bettman/CORBIS, p. 12; © Two Figures on a Boat, 1843 by Auguste Delacroix/Brooklyn Museum of Art/The Bridgeman Art Library, p. 13; © Ivy Close Images/Alamy, p. 14; (right); © iStockphoto.com/Sergii Figurnyi, p. 18 (bottom); © Ron Kimball/www.kimballstock.com, pp. 16, 19; © MIXA RF/Photolibrary, p. 22; © Mark Bond/Dreamstime.com, p. 23 (top/right); © Eti Swinford/Dreamstime.com, p. 23 (Center/right); © iStockphoto.com/Jennifer Sheets, p. 23 (bottom/right); © Richard Nelson/Dreamstime.com, p. 23 (left); © Spyros Bourboulis/First Light/Getty Images, p. 24 (left); © Chuck Pefley/Alamy, p. 26; © Agita Leimane/Dreamstime.com, p. 26 (bottom).

Front Cover: © Fiona Green